# HOOFPRINTS
# ON THE MOON

———————

Ronda Wicks Eller

**HOOFPRINTS ON THE MOON**

Cover graphics and internal artwork by Ronda Wicks

Dedication - Leonard N. Cohen (1934 - 2016)
Dedication - Ruth D. Embling (1942 - 2018)

Eller, Ronda L., 1965 - , author
 -- First edition

Includes index

ISBN-13: 978-0-9809335-8-1

SkyWing Press
12 Quebec Rd., RR5
Clinton, ON, Canada
N0M 1L0

Hoofprints on the Moon is dedicated to the memory of Leonard Cohen (Sept 21, 1934 - Nov 17, 2016)

*C.S. Lewis wrote, "We read to know we're not alone" but I contend that we also write for the same reason despite often being too reticent to make our words 'available for public consumption.*

*The poems in this book deal with love won, lost and reached for but never achieved, intermingled with poems about the soul finding its place in the world and universe. A mix of lyrical, formal styles and free verse make them a unique collection in their own right. They are my tribute to a man whose writings I came to deeply cherish in recent years.*

*Because the primary dedication is to Leonard Cohen, all references to God have been made "G-d" respecting his traditional heritage.*

Hoofprints on the Moon is dedicated to the memory of Ruth D. Batten, m1. Wicks, m2. Embling (Apr 25, 1942 - Sept 17, 2018)

*During the time this manuscript was being compiled, my mother passed away holding onto my hand. A poem I started two months before her death was finished five months later and is included as the first one in this collection. With deepest gratitude for having been blessed with a mom who was my best friend, Hoofprints on the Moon is also dedicated to her, with eternal love!*

*Ronda*

**IMAGE INDEX**

# POEMS INDEX

## POEMS INDEX  continued

## POEMS INDEX continued

**Life Deep-Lived and Wisdom Hard-Earned**

Ruth Dianne Batten (Wicks, Embling) 1942-2018

*for my mother:*

**DEAR MAMA**

Don't take the song from my lips when you go,
leave me a semblance of something I know.
Your temperance, your patience, your gentility
(a song I can cling to with clear memory),

your good, tender heart & your meeker design
are the beautiful tones that all come to mind.
Please don't take the song from my lips when you go,
leave me a semblance of something I know.

When I've known the world to be harsh and cruel,
your love's been my staff as a general rule
and although my strength can hold its own ground
it always finds rest in your song's precious sound.

Oh Mom, leave your song here to harness me
I don't want to stray from your love's symphony.

## HOOFPRINTS ON THE MOON

So smooth, undisturbed, the surface we see
unblemished as it was before the bombardment
of lessons, life meteors, that gored the field or
pock-marked our fleshy, romantic bits— intent
on shaping us with blunted perception.

While you interrogate a broad crater's depth
I scuff dust from a ridge, analyze the raw scar,
to see how upheavals have divided us,
to understand the course your journey took
and leave a mark so you'd know I was there.

All "the greats" have been in this place at some point,
left their flags for tracking— we know by design
that we might find each other if we followed them
while traversing this cold and desolate land
but we are our own hearts and we pace differently.

We thump and we thump, we relentlessly beat
emotion on love's wanting craters and plains,
held fast by past glory's vague remembrance
and driven by echoes of a wandering herd
inscribing fresh hoofprints here on the moon.

## BLACK STALLION

Black stallion of night, glaring at me
from beyond my window sill,
why did you come to seduce me?

*When did I summon this torture*
*of your hoof beats on my heart?*

You flare your nostrils and throw steam
into the cool air of my aloneness.
You make me long for your heat
out of reach and beyond my pane
and I am sadly aware that I cannot
press myself firmly against your flanks
or caress your strong, rippling withers
while measuring your hands with my own.

*Why do you come*
*to seduce me at night*
*while I'm kept*
*under lock and key*
*within my stable?*

## FOR SALE BY OWNER

For Sale By Owner:
BATES MOTEL

   Sprawling, pristine old manor.
   Bed and Breakfast served.
   Income potential:
   You could make a killing!

"Open House Today"

Walk through and view the lovely decor
but avoid the basement
   the stairwell is treacherous:

Imaginations,
  Hallucinations,
    Nightmares,
      Fantasies,
        Memories,
          Visions,
            Dreams
  beyond this point walks a ghostly spirit
  eager to imprison you
  in your own erection.

Caveat Emptor buyer:
    Condition of Sale— AS IS

## MESSAGE TO THE COMPOSER

The note is here
if you're looking for it.

It is carefully tucked away
in your favourite corner
of my grandmother's
hope chest.

It's a pitifully crumpled,
paper butterfly you misplaced
when intrigued by some
less substantial melody.

The note is here, abandoned
but not lost, still holding
the first verse and chorus
in place, clinging
to its last purpose.

Give it a verse to follow
and if not, give it a rest—
permission to stop
its resonant vibrato
and lonely echo.

D.S. al Coda
composer:

The note is here
where you left it—
you haven't finished
the song.

## YOU ALREADY DEPARTED

I lost you
even though the flag was flying.

I searched high among clouds
but they were too bright
and too soft for your thistled feet.

I searched low but the shadows
grew taller than day or night
in your old, flea-bitten alley
yet your absence lingered
in rotted pallets & shipping boxes.

I tried to hold onto you
but the memory folded over
like a wet paper cup.

I called your name and struggled
to keep my flag raised high,
hoping you'd see it and respond
but you had already departed—

gone to experience the world
you didn't know
you'd already become.

## EYE OF JUPITER

I saw you first in a crystal—
the eye of Jupiter revolving,
transforming itself,
becoming earth.

I incubated you
in my young, fertile mind
and we became the baby
and the blessed virgin
but I couldn't contain
your increasing stature.

When you raged and flung
your wild fists at my womb
I knew I had to expel you
or die without expression.

Once in the world
you wandered and returned
after your thirty desert days
to quench your thirst
and clean your hands
at my fountain.

I learned to tolerate the new
haunting way you penetrated
my dreams and grieved
over your baying at the moon
because it failed to satisfy
your unquenchable need for
greater light. Over time

I would've sacrificed myself

to know if you were a god
or demon but I was meant
to be the new Pythia—
I was supposed to understand

your plan to rip my heart
from its fleshy bed
on your way to the cross
before you, whether demon
or god, vanished.

## NO HADRIAN

You don't have to be here
for your breath, lightly grazing
the nape of my neck,
to run its fine fingers over
the course of heightened nerves
leading to the settlement
you made for yourself
in my heart's escarpment.

I don't imagine you know
all these places you live or
how your spirit procreates
subdivisions— multiplying
its hidden web of addresses
in my heart, my mind, my soul.

I merge with you, assuming
only partial ownership,
but you keep drawing me
further from myself.

I will get lost in you here
where no Hadrian Wall
will keep you from claiming
this undiscovered land—

this country of gentle,
undulating chasms.

## STILL

I still feel your warm breath softly
inducing tingles on my neck.
I still feel your musk, your manliness
that stirs my every sense
and your heated flesh engulfing me
as we come close, breast to breast.
I still feel our spirits binding us
together with each kiss.

I still hear your silent whisper
'though you never make a sound
and your eyes still tell the story
of a heart forever bound
to rain on me eternal love,
the same love I give you.
As we live and die should it matter why
you're so much more than memory?

I still feel you holding me.

## SMASH THE DRUM

Tear the hide and smash the drum
that dares to mimic my restless heart.
The drummer is a loathsome idiot
who thinks my anguish is his part.

Take his sticks and let him wander
idle hands to something else
so that my snares be left in silent
listening for my lover's voice!

## SPECTRE

O spectre do not come to me
woeful of what might have been
but from your crystal let me glean
and know events as yet unseen.

Offer your unfettered fortunes
or, by misfortune, opportunity
will never come to you or me—
don't mention that dim reality.

Don't fake your own autonomy,
hovering free o'er stairwell flights,
as if you weren't conjoined to me
and never knew disturbing nights

since I won't buy such disillusion.
We trip on risers, recover and fly.
Your presence is not an intrusion,
     no—
through pleasure and pain we love
     —we sigh.

## BICAMERAL

This face formed inside my head,
owned a voice I could not call
up into the open airway.
It would not speak to me
but with mocking eyes
asked where I was going
and where on earth I'd been?
It suggested I choose
revelation or disillusionment
then looked away,
and I knew it was all
about perspective
when it left me sitting bedside,
my upper lip knit back
against itself—
my tongue too stuck
to speak.

## BEYOND THE COURT

Beyond the court, beyond the aging day,
the sated belly sinks, the room gives way,
yet through it all the soldiers march along
and through it all the drummer's beat goes on.

The drummer and the dreamer pass the pen
with binding beats and wild, erratic bends
slipped into time and season, ever bound
in discourse— lures for the poet-hound.

O hound of ancient corridors you go
to hunt the mice of wisdom gone before,
nose down to scent the sweaty steps of truth
that might lead to the god/dess of your youth.

Your youth— beyond the court when all was clear
and you hadn't yet refined the art of seer,
nor was your heart enshrined within an ode,
your character in rank with bards of old.

With poets old the sated belly sinks,
so when you ask "Why this?" I often think
of roller coasters harnessed to steel rails
while the wild god/dess dodges off at will.

**THE FIST**

Tragically beautiful—
the heart that wrings pain
through a fist of love
and stands beneath grief's umbrella
content that while life
pommels it with rushing torrents,
the puddle's swell
is substance enough.
Tragically beautiful—
the heart that burns away
in awe of passion's raw virginity
alone, too pure to touch,
and so withdraws its hand.

## FROM SHADOWS UNKNOWN

She gathers henbane, hums verses
derived from shadows unknown to most
with her mind hemmed back, stitched
into the place where the man she loves
holds an ancient post.

Her fingers twirl around the bouquet rings
contemplating a wedding troth offered
to the dreamy court in which they danced,
in which they loved before cruel death
jammed the music and tried to blur

his pallid face but left his heart.

## IF ONLY JUST ONE NIGHT

Here beside the brook tumbling from the mount
we wrap our limbs, entwined, among the conifers
and laze away spring days more than we can count
in the disorganized heaping of hoary calendars
or the lunar ebb and tide of primal aquifers.

We connect flickering stars to conjure up a record,
cast our eyes afar to swim within the blue infinity
and with broad strokes reflect in unified accord
on where the mountain's lip meets heaven's deity—
despite the biting wind's green-eyed ferocity.

Beneath the mountain gazing up at summit peak
embedded as the rock, emblazoned by delight,
shifting ecru to mocha and ash in morning's beak,
we will lie here now forever in what remains of night
before we too will lighten and vanish out of sight.

You and I, my love, have achieved this deep erasure
of time and body's airs, of swollen want and need,
the cradling mountain hips coddle us with pleasure
while we moan as naked earth and resurrect the seed
of souls conjoined in love transcendentally!

## LOVE TOO FULL

October days
the cooler nip of winds now
disregard that we're two
well-steeped cups of tea.
They are witnesses
to our copious emptying out,
our full-blown love
too strong to gently weep.
So forever, we utter "goodbye"
and "goodbye" to each other
as we're expelled from the torrid pot
and chilled straight through by icy lips,
consumed and expressed
with only a frail hope of reuniting
somewhere in
"the water works".

## SWEET REFRAIN

Let me be your sweet refrain;
the one that brings you around again.

Let me be the song you sing
that fills the void in everything
you left unsung and left unheard
because you couldn't find the words.

Let me be your sweet refrain.

*Spontaneously written on Cohen's birthday in 2015*

## MY SOUL TO YOUR SOUL

My soul to your soul, your soul to mine,
mingling together, sweeter than wine;
no body required and no parlance due—
my heaven re-merging with all that is you.

My soul to your soul, your soul to mine,
the cosmos inhaling our waters divine
blending of fragrance and Abraham's own
anointed one formed in the mist and the foam

where our souls first kissed
                    and discovered Home.

## LET US NOT BE COUNTED

Let anguish free, let Liberty
spill our blood into the street
to quench the thirsty, riotous mob
while they splatter it with trampling feet.

Let's give the very thing they seek,
be lambs for slaughter on their altar
seeing the holocaust repeat —
men never learn who accost others

*so let us not be counted as aggressors.*

Come my friends, let's light a fire
to warm ourselves while they conspire
and let's mark bull's eyes on our heads,
let's laugh as if already dead

since we, the meek, keep muted voice,
letting radicals besiege our choice
lest we raise a flag or brandish sword,
support a side and fuel the raging horde.

*No, let us not be counted as aggressors.*

## WE TRAVEL LIGHT

We travel light before we're born,
we travel light and then we're shorn
    from places that we used to know
    to places where we have to go.
We try to hold each other near,
we cling to all the memories dear,
    we travel light, conceiving no
    place on earth we'd call our own.
We travel light, leave earthly time
just to escape the pantomime,
    hoping we might hear a sigh
    or that somehow, someday we might
    cross paths again. We travel light.
We set new goals, achieve new heights,
but also know heartbreak and loss,
    stave off the blues, whatever cost.
I've met a few who travel light,
they've helped me pass dark lonely nights,
    but fallen star, you ought to know—
    still traveling light, I'm with you now.
We travel light before we're born,
we travel light and then we're shorn
    from places that we used to know
    to places where we have to go
and when time's up we're pulled away,
pray hard and hope our dreams won't fade.
    We travel light.

*a dance with "Traveling Light", You Want it Darker' album,
by Leonard Cohen, 2016*

## SOUNDS LIKE SONG TO ME

Let the music play again for me,
entreat my ears with your soliloquy—
your resonant harmony
is my eternal rhapsody
and simply spoken
sounds like song to me.

Let the music play again for me.
"Entreat my ears" is my only plea—
my sanctified and sweet refrain,
our holy and unholy domain
simply spoken
sounds like song to me.

## IN CORRIDORS

You came to me. We looked for an exit
but in the dream we couldn't find it
for all the misleading corridors
that challenged us— was there really a door?

Sometimes you left but were still there
in that shifting theater of despair
and sometimes I left although I stayed.
How did we get to be that way?

You came to me. We looked for an exit
but in the dream we couldn't find it
for all of the misleading corridors
that challenged us— was there really a door?

We found ourselves yet somehow missed.
We kissed although we never kissed.
We loved each other word by word
cloaked in tomes— unread, unheard.

Tangle of dreams and tangle of lives
in corridors, a myriad of truth and lies,
our web of faiths and weave confused,
my soul to yours— our love so bruised.

You came to me, we looked for an exit,
but in the dream we couldn't find it
for all of the misleading corridors
that challenged us—
was there ever really a door?

*from a dream circa 1993*

## VILLANELLE FOR HERE AND NOW

The heart rails at what it sees
distraught by divisions and uprising.
The world cries for transparency.
There is no time for complacency
and no advantage in reprising.
The heart rails at what it sees.
When subversive inequality breeds
the stifling result is polarizing.
The world cries for transparency.
Love shrinks from the evil disease
and hate is nurtured in its devising.
The heart rails at what it sees -
it smells the foul air it breathes.
The venal tribe must stop up-sizing.
The world cries for transparency.
Love must be the new increase,
Hate is too demoralizing.
The heart rails at what it sees.
The world cries for transparency.

*a dance with*
*"Villanelle for Our Time",*
*'Dear Heather' album,*
*Leonard Cohen, 2004*

## I MET YOU ON THE LEVEL

I met you on the level,
I bid the white bird call
to offer you my fragrant Rose—
the one we shared before the Fall.

I should have asked "Reply to Sender",
I should have asked you to surrender
but if you came with white flag flying,
how could I know that you weren't lieing?

I met you on the level,
I bid the white bird call
to offer you my fragrant Rose—
the one we shared before the Fall.

We should have stopped the sun from rising
and seized the night, no compromising.
We were always drawn to flesh on flesh
that darkness brought and light repressed.

I met you on the level,
I bid the white bird call
to offer you my fragrant Rose—
the one we shared before the Fall.

If it tortured you, I do regret,
it's just that we could not forget
the others' song or fragrance in the crowd
of people speaking out in tongues
              (speaking far too loud).

I should have asked "Reply to Sender",

I should have asked you to surrender
but we tarried here and hurried there,
you and I— a Wing and a Prayer

pulling up the shadowy darkness,
dragging down the sinewy Light,
trying to connect the force and urge,
trying to put everything right.

I met you on the level,
I bid the white bird call
to offer you my fragrant Rose—
the one we shared before the Fall.

*This poem spring-boarded from the title "On the Level", 'You Want it Darker' album, Leonard Cohen, 2016 but it dances with "Whispers In The Heavens", published in 'Whale Songs in the Aurora Borealis, HMS Press, London, Ontario, 2005.*

## LAST BANJO

I put my money on the banjo,
it was a simple thing to do.
I had to trust the banjo
to see my heartache through.

I saw it closing in on me,
I knew the thing's intent—
my ignorance gutted in its strings,
my wisdom caught in frets.

I don't know how it made its way
through dark, embattled sea,
riding backward winds and waves
to pluck the chords it did in me.

I put my money on the banjo,
it was a simple thing to do,
I had to trust the banjo
to see my heartache through.

I saw it closing in on me,
I knew the thing's intent—
my ignorance gutted in its strings,
my wisdom caught in frets.

*reply to "Banjo",*
*'Old Ideas' album,*
*Leonard Cohen, 2011*

## SOME THINGS

Some things you really can't say to the masses.
some things you simply can't say to yourself.
some journeys don't follow maps or a compass
and where you are headed you never can tell.

Some things are buried too deep to uncover.
History is written for the victor's thrill.
Your quest for answers can go on forever—
the mind may be willing but thoughts distilled.

*Your soul knows desire but it's tainted and mired.*
*Your ancient heart is exhausted and tired.*

Some things only survive under pressure
and some just can't be brought into light.
Some things defy being weighed or measured.
Some things aren't made to surpass the dark night.

You try holding them but they slip away,
try writing them but they come out wrong,
on bent ego and knee you bow down to pray,
for a new start or other divergent song,

*waiting for history to consume its own tail*
*but what lives in abstraction dies in detail.*

Some things you simply can't tell to the minions
and others you can't even say to yourself,
or the one who walks with you in your visions,
his name on your lips and his love on your tongue.

Some loves defy all concise explanation,

some live deeper than time can incise,
developing new inner constellations
that are neither discerned, defined nor devised.

*Some things are diminutive, some need expansion*
*but all keep you shifting between their dimensions.*

Some things only survive under pressure
and some just can't be brought into light.
Sometimes things can't be weighed or measured.
Some are not meant to surpass the dark night.

"Born in Chains"

## NO LOVER

Your lips never dared to kiss me
you filthy, naked refugee.
Your eyes never swam my sea—
no lover ever loved so much of me.

No lover ever loved so much
afraid of tainting what they touched
as you who knew, and you withdrew,
not taking me or leaving you.

Your lips never alit on mine,
your touch never swelled my night,
your lonely heart you laid sublime,
content as shadow in my light

but now you live beyond the veil
and I have missed you even more,
yet you're still here and I can tell
our love has never loved so much before.

## COME HEALING II

Oh undivided Love,
undivided Faith,
come healing of the spirit
in every blessed way.

Come healing of the body
that humbly serves the man,
come healing of the planet,
come healing in the land.

Oh let the heavens hear it—
the heart on bending knee,
come healing of the motive,
come healing of the plea.

Oh undivided purpose,
undivided Love,
come healing of the message
here below and there above.

Come healing of the spirit
that bids each nation rise,
come healing of the sorrow
dripping from each love-torn eye.

Oh let the morning rise now
in perfect harmony,
come healing of the vision
in eyes too blind to see.

Oh undivided Love,
undivided Truth—

come healing of the Tree of Life
half-broken at its root,
come healing of the heartbeat
humbly striving out of sync,
come healing of the music
that trembles out of key.

Come healing of the spirit
in every blessed way,
come healing of the broken prayer
that is the prayer today.

Oh let the heavens hear it—
the heart on bending knee,
come healing of the motive,
come healing of the plea.

Come healing of the spirit
in every blessed way,
come healing of the broken prayer
that is the prayer today.

*inspired by "Come Healing",*
*'You Want it Darker' album,*
*Leonard Cohen, 2016*

## DIGGING UP THE HEART

Here I am in the garden
and I'm digging up the heart,
the one I buried long ago.
I'm digging up the heart—

the one that longed to keep you,
the one that broke apart.

I'm standing in the garden
considering what's gone on—
I can't forget the torment
when you left on your mission

swearing that our love would last
through reward or prohibition.

I dropped that blood-soaked pump
and let it flounder on terrain
to enlist an eager shovel
and dredge out the miry clay.

I recall its panicked shrieking
when I interred it there that day

and the bird that sang a dirge
while sitting lofty on its nest,
flinging wiry little scraps at me
in its own outraged protest.

Now I stand here at the same spot,
destitute of all pretense

and recount how it all happened,
how everything went wrong,
but about that cocky fowl—
I don't recollect its song.

It's been ages since you've been here,
eons now since you've been gone

but I hear that poor thing pleading,
somehow I knew right from the start
that I would miss its woeful heaving
so I'm digging up my heart.

## BE I OPHELIA OR CRAZY JANE, IN FOUR ACTS

Act One:

'If music be the food of love'
'To be or not to be'—
my thousand ducat wealth
I would surrender happily.

Long live the days I witnessed pass
since Hamlet's soliloquy—
be I Ophelia or Crazy Jane,
the name means naught to me.

The tides that bear up lovers bold
all turn against them too;
if music be the food of love
its rhythms must pursue

the change proclaimed in every tide,
tasting sweet or sour through,
maddening every mortal sense,
re-colouring every hue.

'To be or not to be' I ask—
my true love slain by poison's bite,
insanity wed to the living dead,
his kingdom slipped into the night.

*Darkness cannot make it right.*

Act Two:

Were Hamlet here, upon my lap
his head would not be lain.
Beneath his window where I stood,
yes, there I would remain

and maiden, I'd as maiden stay,
while he, in vital solitude,
expunged the wiles of vengeful ways
until his vices were subdued.

Were Hamlet here, oh, only if
his lot weren't cast afar
he would've known my love surpassed
the harlot and the whore.

And crazy as the world may be,
moreso, it always is,
he might have lived with my mad legs
sweetly entwined in his

but, like my father, he is gone,
in truth I am gone too—
were it to be or not to be
we paid the court its due.

*We were just passing through.*

Act Three:

If music be the food of love
I'm starved, my bones are bare.
Jack the Journeyman is dead,
he's neither here nor there.

As Crazy Jane I bed that man
absent as G-d above
in whom all things remain indeed,
including absent love.

As Ophelia I must confess
that women's skirts don't float
but did I care? No, not at all,
while life was fading out

for sing I did and sing I will
of wild Jack upon that hill
and how he meant to ravage Jill
after Jane, that ne'er-do-well!

But now I cannot eat a bite
of what my love has kept from me,
for want of Hamlet I'm contrite
and I keep to my window seat

in heaven, what chaotic place,
my spirit's with the sentry,
I'm not quite sure it's paradise
but it is where we gain entry.

Forsooth he'll be no lunatic when
he comes but most assuredly
he'll act deranged as hatters do
who've breathed in too much mercury.

So herein lies the matter:
death does seem the best recourse
and what a shame it ends this way
to mute the bishop's chatter—

    *'though I'm sure that cleric's madder.*

Act Four:

Was it to be or not to be?
That's the fitting question.
Was it nobler to suffer love
not loving once in session

or in Jack's bed feign wild passion?
'All things remain in G-d'
or nobler yet, in Ophelia fashion
to use an unplanned suicide

and drown inside the thirsty pool?
or perhaps thrash wild arms
against the swilling vacuum's tug
and bellow out a fool's alarm?

Am I now where I should've been?
Was it real or truly just a dream
or in the dream of Hamlet's queen?
Could life be just one single theme?

We're queen! Ophelia, Jane come forth!
I've set the twisted thing to reason—
'To be or not to be' conforms
itself to every season

*and your bishop calls it treason!*

*This poem twists aspects of "Hamlet's soliloquy", "Hamlet and Ophelia" and "Twelfth Night" by Wm. Shakespeare, "Crazy Jane, Jack the Journeyman and the Bishop" by Wm. Yeats, and "Passing Through" by Richard Blakeslee, arr: Leonard Cohen, 'Live Songs' album, 1973 to present a new, unique theme.*

## REPROACH

Who led you to my temple?
Who offered you my hand
and the right to claim my body
as your private promised land?

Who made my breasts your altar,
made me wear your yoke and halter
and told you it was right to worship
night after sweat-drenched night

after night?

Who offered you my temple
to harness at your whim,
to perform your drunken ritual
and embalm me from within?

There is no bridle needed
to restrain a broken host
consigned to your conceited
and vile, unholy ghost

but be careful how you boast.

You've turned love into disgust
let there be no more confusion
I will no longer be the altar
of your self-obsessed delusion.

## LETTERS

Someone's been playing
with the old Smith-Corona
in the corner.

They've been typing letters
about you— no, wait,
they're your letters.

Take them with you
if you want;
I made copies already
and have wall space
waiting to be decorated
with any part of you
I can recover—

understanding
the way you beg
to be framed.

## LETTERS 2

lips cease, my love, words do not obey -
they live in letters. I do too.
I kiss your lips, your mind, and all
your nakedness with meaning,
while spaces between add increase
to your perfected heart and soul.
shall we let life burn us on the page?
should we not, instead, be framed?

## THE SONG OF ABRAHAM

I put that axe in the clay god's hand
after I slew his clay god kin
and tried to scrub my father clean.
It shed no tears— that breathless idol,

that piece of idle handiwork.
I knew my father's sin but worse
was that it was not his alone.
How merciful the nameless One

that came to judge my forlorn heart,
to rescue me and write new laws
within my soul, in every part
intent on having me progress.

*For me that was the blessing.*

But now the laws are smashed in two—
my heart is sacrificed in Schechem
where I take refuge, every atom
in earth, inside G-d's ancient bosom,

between Ebal's peak and Gerizim's
with love and hate both out of reach;
I cannot suckle, I cannot feast
yet struggle with dichotomies.

*For me, that is the curse.*

The blessings leave when I curse the divide,
the curses burn when my blessings rise—
caught between the blessing and curse
I'm unsure what's better and what is worse,

I gamble with faith that my G-d is real
and my suffering has preserved the deal,
but it's not just mine, no, we're all caught
between blessings and the curses bought.

*For me, that is the blessing.*
*For me, that is the curse.*

## WERE YOU THERE?

Did I impale you during the dark ages
when we couldn't see each other
for shadows?

Did I fail to laugh at your reckless jokes
or offer a gold crown's pay
for your courtly entertainment?

I know I ordered an invasion
and torching of some remote desert camp.
Were you there?

Did you know it was me
when you raped and left my body
half-dead in the street?

Was it you who stole my child to enslave?

How could we carry such insights
this far for enlightening?

We assumed they'd die with us
but now we know that nothing dies

and having learned to love
is there a shovel sturdy enough
to dig us one last hole?

## PACT

I don't want your wine or biscuit
so let's make a pact:
you keep yours and I'll keep mine.

Let's feast together, and
each consume our own
so nothing pure chances tainting
even if nothing tainted
gains redemption.

*We can hold the status quo*
*and leave the alchemy to G-d.*

Between you and I,
there was never a marriage
and this is no reception.

I don't know who's better off
but I don't need another saviour.
You're not Jesus, and let's face it:

we've been baptized so often
our scaly skin sheds pale flakes
as a disregarding sacrifice on the altar.

*We know the snake still slithers here—*
*so let's leave the alchemy to G-d.*

## THE MARTYRS

We've died so many times
and the crucifixion's done,
our flesh is cracked and broken,
our wine skin's ready to burst.
We are so well fermented
the ground can't hold the sum
of our over-ripened blood
but the Messiah's blend is here
to resurrect us from within
so get out the pewter cups—
let the honeymoon begin.

## FIRE OF THE SOUL

At night I hear its flame
and crackle with each spark
while its bed feeds on your name
enshrined by ashes in my heart.

There's an air somewhere that feeds it
and vague memories that relieve it,
in the dead of night I know
it is a fire of the soul.

It's a fire of the soul
and a fever of the mind,
it's a never-ending heartache
with a sense of the divine

and it's not that I'm unworthy
or that in Hell I've been assigned,
no, I've feasted here with Mercy
and with Grace I have reclined

but you are the missing element
in this busted soul design,
the stubborn flame's relentless—
I still burn to make you mine.

## TRYING TO SING

What is time
but a villainous executioner
and what is this song
if not massacred
lacerated chords bleeding
discordant harmonies
that drift through your day
and get lodged in my night
where you signal autumn
and I live throughout winter;
my white bones shivering
without your sun-bronzed cover
because time flayed you away
and left us both disfigured
on the knife-laden scaffold
of seasons, to everything
there is a season, still
trying to sing, still
praying for salvation,
becoming
dust.

**BREAK FREE**

It's just another day coming to call,
used to mean something, now nothing at all.
I always thought love would bring you to me
but love's still entrenched in its own mystery:
one foot in the present, one in history
trying to move forward, trying to break free,
always strong in heart but weak in the knee.

My faith was blind in youth but now I can see
the man that you were, always looking for me,
praying I'd follow your sad love song home
but where were you then, if not lost and alone
on your chair by the window, the muses' stage,
penning the upsurge of an illumined New Age
while your soul slipped on and off the page?

Now every morning that breezes in calls
with its own invention or nothing at all
and you never found me, I never found you;
love kept getting stuck in the hullabaloo.
I always thought love would bring you to me
but love, on its own, could never break free—
it was too obstructed. We were too blind to see.

## SCREAM

Circumscribed by the reins of night
I scuff against the darkened veil,
bereftly stare into the chasm—
my soul biting at cold silence.
This stable, this old stall, emptier
now than when you were here
(but thousands of miles away).
Fettered by the reins of night
I bray defiance to the lantern's flame
and scream for your return
so I can either sleep in my harness
or burn the structure down.

## ONION LOVE

Our love is an onion—
its skin finally peeling
in a sheeted falling-away
ritual, well-weathered
and bruised by time.
It's ready to be opened,
to surrender its succulent,
sap-streaming core
if we only spirit up
passion's honed blade,
cut through layer on layer,
chisel out the heart's
ensconcement
of absolute pain
and consummate ecstasy
in savoury kisses so pure,
so potent and so mature
we cannot help
but cry.

## PRIMORDIAL GENESIS

Our fire danced with water,
our existence spun around
and conceived its own ignition
through a potent hissing sound

carried on air's virgin current,
knit by us with tumbling wings,
we harnessed light to matter,
spawned great earth imaginings.

Our rapture spiked the heavens,
our flames impaled the deep,
our passion knit both seedlings
in earth's recumbent sleep.

In wedded blissfulness we grew
magnificent, divine,
rhapsodic and profuse within
our souls by Source Design!

## WE'VE BOTH BEEN HERE BEFORE

There is no more time love,
in this place there is no more;
our private cloister's open
beckoning us through its door

and we know the gasps still swirling
breathless in the corridor
and it's okay, okay love,
we've both been here before.

Here in the darkest corners,
here in the vibrant light
we've been hot and cold and tepid,
we've been wrong and we've been right,

we've aped the timorous ostrich
been propelled in phoenix flight,
braced our sails on wild white wave caps
scaled the craggy mountain height.

Our entanglement's okay love,
it could never be more right,
time's a feeble thought in shackles—
we've outgrown both day and night.

We've purported throne and scepter,
we donned old tattered clothes,
bloodied swords in vengeance
and then faced our hearts in woe.

We pled forgiveness in the transept
and humbly threw our gavels down
for the fools who would retrieve them,
assuming they should wear the crown.

Now we dance in full soul essence
where divisions can't be found,
welcomed twins within the heavens
where impassioned joys abound.

No perilous vice can thwart us;
on our hearth they bide no more,
our citadel's wide open,
offering union at its core.

We bore every gasp still swirling
in this hollow corridor
hallowed through our marriage,
Love, we've both been here before.

## QUIETUDE

I come to you in quietude
like a spider in its web
awaiting love's sweet morsel,
longing to be fed,
longing to enfold you
within my plasma rays,
to adios this yearning
and embrace more sated days.

I come to you in quietude
like sunset on the sea,
faithful to my promise
that when you long for me
I'll kiss your deepest eye pools
with warmth and sheer delight,
invest your dreams with comfort
that we're going to be alright.

I come to you in quietude
with one desire to be
there and holding you,
while you are there
and holding me.

## DAIMON SONG

You were the Sky when I was the Earth.
I was the Womb and you were the Birth.
You were the Eagle and I was the Dove.
I was the Fragrance but you were the Love.
You grew into Thorn when I turned Rosen.
I became Gentile when you were The Chosen.
You were the Shepherd while I was the Lamb,
I shone as the Sun when you were the Moon.
When you were the Sword I served as the Salve
and I was the Hero while you were the Slave.
You sought Gehenna and I, the Baptism;
I became the Cross you shaped as my Chisel.
Now you live in Death and I die in Life
but you are my Husband and I am your Wife
spiraling around the Immense Axiom
of Darkness and Light, what's Right & what's Wrong,
of Daimon and Daimon, the Two that are One.

## BEFORE YOU WROTE

I don't need to decode your cries
for justice, peace and virtue,
for broken love made wholesome love.
I know the nights you wept through.

I knew them well before you wrote
your epilogue, your Old News,
the arching Bridge, the Motherland,
what was true but only half-true.

I don't need to decode your cries
in layered compositions—
separate hearts all bleed the same
inside The Great Condition.

## IN MY MUSINGS

Whispering and murmurs
of other lifetime things,
your face drawn into pictures,
white horses with great wings,
a Buddha in my musing,
vague pictures in my mind—
these murmurings and whispers
will not leave me behind.
Milestones and markers,
clues too broad to see,
rhymes in rare brochures,
your face on magazines,
Buddha's waltz, the girl's round,
the slouching beast, poetic moan
are all mystique and milestones
that won't leave me alone.
Photographs and memories
were Croce's old lament,
we had more subtle casualties
in our love tournament.
Vent of tears and well of laughs,
disconnected synchronism—
those memories and photographs,
this New World cynicism.
A Buddha in my vespers,
vague pictures in my mind—
this whispering, these murmurs
will not leave me behind.

## I AM AN OUTCAST

I am an outcast.
You made me that way
by launching love's lost arrows
sharp - then sharper -
trying to expose me,
to draw me out of my crowd
and whether it was by
my scream of excitement
or pain didn't matter.
You filled me with holes—
gaping wounds that I scrambled
to bandage, even as
you stuck a hand in one,
then another, your head
and penis trying to climb inside
for a look at my thoughts
and a feel for my barrenness;
the lassitude of dreams
in my heart and lethargy
of my innocent love.
How could I not scream
after so many attempts
at penetration?
I saw the watching crowd
plug their ears, attempting
to avoid the obvious truth
that I am so much your outcast
I can't even hold my tongue.

## LOVE IS A WOMAN

Love is a woman.

The moon is a woman
with a man inside it

and if that doesn't
say something
nothing will.

## THANK YOU FOR THE POETRY

Thank you for the poetry
and pictures that you drew.
They arrived a little late—
lost in the mail I suppose.

Your mother came to visit.
She said you started the collection
before you ever met me
and that she didn't know
you could call up the past;

she thought you were wedged
until she found you scrying
and you shared your discovery
that the time line was skewed.

Your father came to visit.
He said your mother grieved like Mary
over her firstborn son's misfortune
but he assured she was no virgin.

He added that you left for the war
like all good homeland lads
even though you knew you'd die.

So thank you for the songs
declaring all your love
and the sketches of me too.

They're splattered with red blotches
and I can't help but wonder
if it's your blood — or mine.

## ONE BREATH

We are one breath from life to life,
one letter and that letter's twin,
a mirrored breath and breath combined,
a barely distinguished inhalation,
one undetermined exhalation.
And 'tho the generations change
we keep our place, maintain our mission
inside the word, the great symposium—
eternal monologue of soul.

We bend and twist, reshaped to fit
within time's passing overlap
like hummingbird-in-motion's striking
blur, or heated tongues colliding
to twist to blend then subdivide
dominant and submissive traits
inside the forge. We know dualism
all firsthand, having established
confluent and divergent natures:

fueling love with sweet rose nectar
while burning hearts to ashen mulch
and the universal choir sings
while the simple world chatters on...

# A NEW MEMORIUM

I know our Love, I know its day
from life to life, its errant way—
its tragedy I can't forget,
how Fortune with Misfortune met.

It rose and rose through darkest night,
was cleaved in half but finding light
resolved to become whole again
and traveled out to find its twin.

On raging sea it pled with G-d,
was drowned, reborn, and earth it trod
but found no substance in the land
and weak with hunger couldn't stand.

On buckled knee it learned to pray,
at war with Ego all the way,
intent to be with you my Love,
not knowing you were cast above

beyond the Veil. My forlorn soul
resumed its quest for you below
among dear hearts that never knew
the sorrowed plight of One made Two.

My forty days spent in one hour
and thousand hours in one bower;
bower of bowers a forest wide
devised to hold me, caught inside.

In tall grass blades the beetle weaves,
the snake slithers, caterpillar sleeps
and I among them shrunk so small
but aimed to rise above them all.

Each raindrop covered me in pools,
the babbling brook absorbed all fools;
from it I managed to keep clear
quite sure I'd never find you there.

Damp dried in new sun I despaired
among the creatures gathered there
but a meadowlark sang out one´eve
when I had no hope but believe

that where you dwelt her music played
to lead you here, into my glade.
I know you heard, I know you moved,
I felt your soul swell in my Love.

I waited but you never came,
my heart went wild without your name,
without its own, obscured by earth,
where nothing recognized its worth.

The day grew long, the night set in
I petitioned G-d to start again
but truth presided in my soul:
I must be rent to become whole.

O Love, the next thing I recall
was being there, beyond the Veil
my soul ballooned outside, inside
its shell, for hope I'd be your bride

again. Oh I could feel you close—
our Love forever overflows!

Anon I learned you had just gone
to find me in that wretched throng.

Again I could not get to you
but now and then I've seen you through
some trials I've already faced
when I was there, inside that place.

Until We Meet Again

## THAT'S WHAT THEY TOLD ME

It must have hurt when I wasn't listening
and everyone heard you but me.
I never knew I was transgressing,
I sincerely thought I was free
because that's what they told me—
　　　*yeah, that's what they said.*

I remember when we strolled all evening,
the moon kissing us through the trees,
me lost in your voice and missing the meaning
"Unyielding Love can be deceiving"
or that's what they told me—
　　　*yeah, that's what they said.*

If I could translate what went unspoken,
word for word in every degree,
I wonder if I wouldn't feel so broken
since "I'm not supposed to be free",
at least that's what they told me—
　　　*yeah, that's what they said.*

I know sorrow despite all our dreaming,
we used to be greater than sky,  land or seas
riding a wave that was all-encompassing
"but Love is a trying disease".
That's what they told me—
　　　*yeah, that's what they said.*

I said they were bonkers, I wasn't myself,
but now I stare at your hat on my shelf
collecting dust, in want of your head,
while I sit disillusioned on the old bed,

crafting words that might've been said
if only we'd been free instead
                of maddening in Love.

## RESTLESS HEART

Restless heart, O restless mind
when will you stop, be satisfied
like those around who seem content?
Why must you churn until you're spent?

And will you stop when in your grave
or still find something else to crave,
some thing to seek, some thought to own?
Will you move on if left alone?

O restless heart, when flesh is gone
what appetite will spur you on?
Nomadic soul with gypsy feet,
when will your travels be complete?

You beat my breast from inside out
attempting to bust free no doubt
but never seem to find relief—
why can't you simply let things be?

What curious blood, what ravenous soul,
sojourner, now where did you go
devouring life to feed your pen?
I see that you've run off again.

## KISS ME

North to my south,
east to my west,
love of my life
you are the best.
Night to my day,
fall to my spring
you are my joy
in everything.

Kiss me today,
kiss me tonight,
kiss me tomorrow,
kiss me for life.

Breath to my breath,
my bosom's sway,
kiss me tomorrow,
kiss me today.
Heart to my heart,
my bosom's sigh,
kiss me tomorrow,
kiss me tonight.

We survived Nuremberg,
we survived Rome,
Normandy's shores
could not send us home.
Pompei singed our hands,
we put Troy to bed,
the Sahara was murder
but we rose again.

Oh kiss me today,
kiss me tonight,
kiss me tomorrow,
kiss me for life.

Breath to my breath,
our soul's old and grey,
come kiss me tomorrow,
kiss me today!

## I LOVED YOU FROM A DISTANCE

I loved you from a distance
'cause you needed to be free,
that's how it always was
between the likes of you and me;

Sugar Bay in Montserrat
and our tempest in the tea—
you warred against my breast
but I massaged your feet.

I loved you from a distance
'tho I kissed a vent or two—
I knew, despite your fever,
you'd enjoy my residue.

I soothed your deep foundation
from inside my buffer zone,
relieved  internal pressure
and reminded you of home.

I never got to hold you
or caress your weary head;
from here, inside my harbour,
I absorbed your tears instead

and when, by moon, I crested,
I felt the great increase
of your volcanic, weeping love
in passionate release.

You stood against the hurricanes,
balanced my rising tide,
extruded soft stone pillows
to rest with me,  your  bride;

my body always rocked against
your andesitic shore,
loving from a distance.
I could never touch your core.

I loved you from a distance
'cause you needed to be free,
your magmatic moods required
it, not hospitality,

and eventually you understood
the way our lot was cast.
I was first to love you
and I would be the last.

## TRIPTYCH

The call to prayer is over,
the choir has moved on;
I don't know why you came here
or why I'm still alone,

why the altar's made of marble
or some unyielding stone.
Why couldn't it be softer?
Why can't we take it home?

We used to have a chapel
here, on our castle grounds;
I don't know where it went to
or where its love is now,

why you grew trees  around it
to hide it from my view,
why the call to prayer was over
when my search found it anew.

I don't know why you sabotaged
our humble synagogue;
you made it  cold and barren—
it's inglorious and wrong

with eroded triptych pillars
and hearts drowned in the font,
the holy chancel wringing out
such forlorn pain and want

but the call to prayer is over
and the choir has gone home;
it's  you and I alone here—
just us and this old koen.

Why can't we resurrect it?
It's still vaguely intact.
Why obstruct the one thing
you keep praying to come back?

## SWIMMING

I swam inside your blue eyes,
I floundered at the pass
when I chose to dive, oh never
did I reach for a compass,

did I think it was forever
until now, when looking back
and seeing I stayed so long
I was rippling in the past.

The days, they entered creeping,
then rushed out in a blur
'til age dug up the remnant
of our bones, expelled the cur

that stole our ancient wisdom,
kept as prizes for a time.
I lapsed into it yesterday
in the stream of some reprise

and like a photo captured
saw me swimming in your eyes.

## SKETCHY VIGNETTES

i.
I draw your eye —
that place
where I'm the pupil
who never goes out
for recess and you,
the teacher, gives
the lesson plan
before we switch
positions.
You know the drill—
we're creatures of habit.

ii.
I draw your mouth
as silent as the days
that made it mute but
left you a clearer voice
than any other, and
a breath that winds
gently back to mine.

iii.
Sometimes
I draw caricatures
you made of yourself,
not to master
your technique
but to find myself
in the mood.
I leave those ones
half-finished—
like us.

iv.
Other people draw you
with a head, body,
Background & props
trying to envelop you,
but not me—
I shape an eye,
a mouth and a hand
in different sittings,
trying not to get lost.

v.
I redraw another artist's
caricature of you,
because he's impartial
and I'm not...
but I only replicate ones
that capture your essence.
I'm more of a connoisseur
than you.

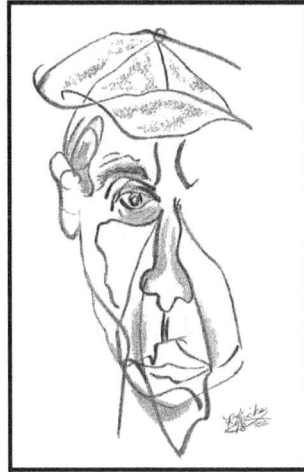

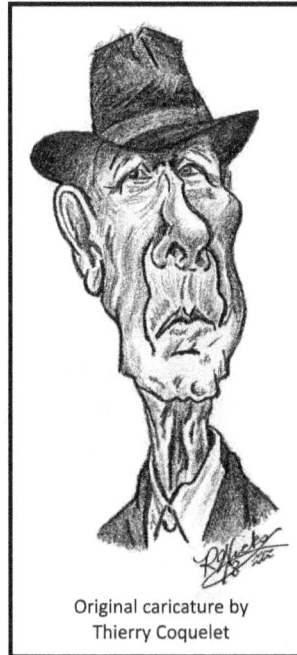

Original caricature by
Thierry Coquelet

## UNREQUITED

I remember
how we stopped, knee deep
in the snow-dropping woods
and I let you draw me close,
your lips sweetening
your pledge of eternal love.

*Did you even speak*
*before I fully tasted them?*

*Did you never think*
*they might not wear off?*

I remember
marrying someone, but not you,
and the company you joined
to witness our nuptials,
how before the dour vicar
my lips still pined for yours

but received instead,
a mellifluous kiss
that soured me for life.

*(from a dream)*

## INNER SANCTUM

Between night and day
an uneasy truce sets
and rises, and at twilight
the everlasting voices
are magnified
on the drowsy lake
of nether consciousness.

We cling to each other
and wait for immortals
of the Inner Sanctum
to teach us what they will.

Between past and present
an uneasy truce rises
and sets, and at twilight
we hear ourselves
answering
through words
of ancient stone.

## SWEET NOTHING

I went out to the cliff,
I couldn't take the street,
I wanted to breach the place
where earth and water meet,
where ailing hearts desire
to enter something new
and trade this world for something
akin to solitude.
I stared at the expanse,
threw off my shoes behind,
raised hands in soul defiance
as my step divorced the land.
Surrendered to her air
my wings fumbled about,
she tried to buoy me there
but I was too dense to float,
then she blew sweet nothing—
sweet nothing was the thing
I couldn't hold for trying
more than anything.
My heavy-weighted mind
was a shroud I couldn't shake—
I was the wrong design
and I died to know my grave.
Now here I am again
where ailing hearts desire
but I'm learning how to fly
like a moth into the fire!

## FROM ONE TABLE TO ANOTHER

I found your little messages
scrawled on all the serviettes
strewn across the cafeteria.
In one you remembered
what it was all about
and in one you forgot
to finish the sentence.

You called them truths
but you were full of shit
and sometimes you even dared
to expound, confessing it.
On one you drew random circles
and dots around David's Star
as if I would or even could
connect them to mirror you—
knowing you couldn't
do it yourself.

I thought you came here to eat.
You said you were famished
but then you abandoned food
and turned these napkins
into paper prayers.
Was the food so unsavoury
or did you forget to stop
begging G-d's blessing
on your dissatisfaction
between one table and another
before you gave up the Ghost
and vanished?

## ALEXANDRIA

The swords and the screams
turned our nightmares
to dreams.
How did we meet
such a tragic end?
Oh brother, dear brother,
my love and my friend!
There's a tunnel here
and a dank room there,
and bones everywhere
to take if you care
from an underground
where conspirators strove
to send us through death
to heaven above.
Alexandria knew
we were joined at the heart,
Why did it have to
tear us apart?

*(from a dream)*

## REVERIE

A song for the man and his company—
the booze and the women, the great reverie
he used to surround the tragedy
of a heart half made of stone.

> *He got away with murder, he got away with love,*
> *he got away with accolades for songs to G-d above.*

A song for the man and his fire,
his passion and pain, his burning desire,
his urge to be chorus, conductor and choir
with a heart dipped half in the stream.

> *He got away with murder, he got away with love,*
> *he got away with accolades for songs to G-d above.*

His words were mixed like potions,
his songs - enchanted spells,
he thrilled the devil so much
he got a special place in Hell.

> *He got away with murder, he got away with love,*
> *he got away with accolades for songs to G-d above*

But G-d could not divorce him—
he got a seat in Heaven too,
and roses came from people
he knew… and never knew.

> *He got away with murder, he got away with love,*
> *he got away with accolades for songs to G-d above*

A song for the man and his muses,
his success and his abuses,
his disciplines and misuses—
that aspiring infidel!

## SOMEONE

someone told me not to write like you
everyone writes like someone

> *there is nothing new*
> *under heaven and earth*

but i don't always write like you
I change my clothes regularly too

> *cleanliness is next to G-dliness*

there's no trademark on colour or culture
nobody owns universal consciousness

> *there is one body and one Spirit*

someone should tell you not to write like me
but why? we don't care if we write alike

> *imitation is the best form of flattery*

somebody should tell someone to shut up

> *nobody will*

## RIPPLING SEA

Shadow on the rippling sea,
sign of something  obscure
below the surface—
may be driftwood,
may be love
down deep.
See?

## FINAL WALTZ

I've danced with other men before
   for you I walk,
my dancing shoes are packed away
   beside my frock.

You came and swept me off my feet,
   rose on the stage
and didn't miss a single beat
   each move you made.

My dancing stage is vacant,
   the waltz is through,
I gave my dance to other men,
   myself to you.

## DANCE OF ONE

Alone in the night I lay dreaming
we're dancing neath silhouette moon
and I look in your eyes as you shed your disguise
midst the scattering of each twilight hue.

Your hands touch my back e'er so softly,
my heart shivs in your sweet embrace,
and I reach for your name as you smile once again
with emotions no word can replace.

In the eve our lives vary in meaning,
true expressions of love are unplanned
and the mind can't reprove what the spirit makes move
in the heart of a woman and man.

We step to the tune of our passion,
unaware of a present or past,
and we merge into one as the magic is done
causing each sacred moment to last.

We waltz in the Garden of Eden,
respecting our Danger of Need,
and I flow back into you reuniting the two—
with fervour for life I'm received.

Alone in the night we incarnate
manifesting the truth we both know:
we were Woman and Man when the world first began
the Dance of One Eternal Soul.

# THE NAMELESS ONE
A One-Scene Play by Ronda Wicks Eller, 2008

## Cast of Characters:

Three Magi *(in purple cloaks with gold trim, holding scrolls and candlesticks)*
Animus Mundi *(person with head of a brown falcon, flowing brown robes)*
Spiritus Mundi *(person with the head of a white falcon, flowing white robes)*
Angel *(holding a long sword and/or sceptre)*
Child *(in pajamas)*
4 Creepers *(children in hooded, black capes)*

**Setting:**

Stage is vacant except for one child's bed at the center. All events take place around the bed (Magi behind the bed, Spiritus Mundi on left side and Animus Mundi on right side of bed)... except where otherwise indicated.


***Curtains Open***

First Magi *(chanting)*:

We sing praises— we sing...
Hallelujah to the nameless one!
We know Him in our hearts,
we know Him... we know Her!

Second Magi *(chanting)*:

Our souls connect— we sing,..
our blood cries out with joy,
loving joy singing through!
We feel every embrace
every moment of knowing

Third Magi *(chanting)*:

We know— we hope
to know Him... to know Her more,
always more... we sing!

Spiritus Mundi *(enters from left side of stage and speaks in a narrative voice)*:

The trees bow down their heads and listen to the wind sighing through the heavy womb, whistling hymns from the rock of ages. The black Madonna carries her child upon the earth and the oceans roar. The powerful music of Seraphim waters the soulful gardenia. Fertilizing over-spray kisses us, the blessed shale, and caresses our desire!

Second Magi *(chanting)*:

And we sing— higher, ever higher!
We sing to the holy mountain,
we praise its boundless majesty.

Third Magi *(chanting)*:

Praise Him— praise Her
our voices lifting, our eyes fixed
on the heavens, on the Light
of His being, of Her being!

First Magi *(chanting)*:

We sing our longing— our belonging!
We adore the spirit of the Nameless One.
Hallelujah!!!

Animus Mundi *(enters from right side of stage and speaks in a narrative voice)*:

The songbirds rise from their nesting places to join the orchestration, to lend their winged notes, to channel the Nameless One through their tiny chambers and the running deer stop to listen, to pay tribute through the art of being still, knowing calm and speaking a peace beyond words, the knowing of an untouchable spirit that touches everything, that is all-encompassing!

*(Lights dim as Spiritus Mundi exits left side of stage, Animus Mundi exits right side of stage and the Magi leave centrally, through the back curtain as a child enters near the front of the stage and kneels by the bed, preparing to pray; lighting increases to a half-lit level)*

Child *(praying)*:

Now I lay me down to sleep
I pray thee Lord my soul to keep
safely held within thy Light
as I slumber through the night.

Bless my soul with peace I pray
and go with me through each new day
armed with dreams and focus clear
to inspire me while living here.

Now I lay me down to sleep
and as I close these peepers
dear G-d, I pray and bid you keep
me safe from dream-thief creepers!

*(Lullaby Music plays in the background as the child crawls into bed and goes to sleep; A short silence follows the lullaby and then a group of Creepers creep in, two from each side, mumbling)*

First Creeper *(right side, all other creepers quietly mumbling in the background)*:

We're gonna get you if it takes all night.
Your spirit's strong and rather bright.
We're here to steal away your dreams
because we want their lovely beams.

Second Creeper *(left side, all other creepers quietly mumbling in the background)*:

We live out in the old, dark void,
a world your unnamed G-d destroyed,
we have no dreams but what we steal
and we want yours— we make no deal!

*(The child sits up in the bed, sees the creepers and speaks to them)*

Child *(glancing back and forth between the creepers on each side)*:

Who are you that come to me
as dark as any darkness be?
You're not from here, Oh, I can tell,
but I don't fear your nasty spell.

*(the child looks up and folds hands in prayer)*

Child *(praying again)*:

Our Father, who art in heaven,
Hallowed be thy name
Thy kingdom come, Thy will be done...

*(An angel appears from the back, center of the stage and a bright light instantly shines down from above onto the child and angel together)*

Third Creeper *(right side; slowly backing away with the other creepers)*:

Get that light away from us,
it's more than bright, it's hurting us!
It is that Nameless One again,
His angel's here to stop our fun!!!

*(creepers mumble in the background)*

Fourth Creeper *(left side; all still backing away)*:

Well we'll be back when you're off guard
you pleasant child, it may be hard
We won't give up, you count on that—
we want your visions, we'll be back!

*(the creepers finish backing off the stage and the angel leaves toward back, center stage)*
*(Spiritus and Animus Mundi and the Magi return)*

Third Magi *(chanting)*:

We sing praises— we sing
Hallelujah to the Nameless One!
We know Him in our hearts…
know Him, know Her.
Our souls connect— we sing!

First Magi (chanting):

We come to Him with joy,
Her loving joy sings through!
We feel every embrace,
every moment of knowing too.

Second Magi (chanting):

We know He shines in us,
She shines in us
more, always more—
We sing!

(the child twirls around victoriously, then stops and stands still, as if in a daze)

Spiritus Mundi (speaks in narrative while the child slowly goes back and lays down to sleep again, as if sleepwalking):

The young child lays down and sleeps, peacefully unaware that (his/her) spirit had ever arisen or that the Nameless One answered when called upon by sending one of his loyal defenders. And the archangels lift their voices, they praise Him, they praise Her whose power and Light emanates through them, whose power protects the praising, prayerful ones!

Animus Mundi (spoken narrative):

The night lies down its head and sleeps beneath the stars, reflecting the child's spirit, reflecting the spirit of the Nameless One who watches through the owl's eye and sings with wolfish voice; the moon, like a lighthouse, glows 'til dawn when the nameless one will shine instead, through rays of brilliant sun to light our waking minds, dovish with love and peaceful goodwill!

First Magi *(chanting)*:

And we sing higher— ever higher!
We sing to the holy mountain,
we praise its boundless majesty.
We praise Him, praise Her...

Second Magi *(chanting)*:

our voices lifting— our eyes fixed
upon the heavens, upon the light
of His being, of Her being
we sing

Third Magi *(chanting)*:

our longing!
Our own belonging!
We adore the Holy Spirit
of the Nameless One!!!

*Magi together say:*
Amen.

*Spiritus and Animus Mundi with Magi all bow their heads and
 the lights dim.*


**The curtains close.**

## LIFE DEEP-LIVED AND WISDOM HARD-EARNED - REVIEW

The poems in Hoofprints On The Moon are testimony to the inquiring heart of Ronda Wicks Eller.  These are poems born from a life deep-lived and wisdom, hard earned.

Eller is a courageous poet, unwilling to confine herself, in style or subject, and her poems fearlessly chart the loss of loved ones, the longing for intimacy, and the hope for redemption.  Centuries swirl together in Eller's poetic landscape, myths walk beside old lovers and geography is fluid, lending a delightful timelessness to her work and allowing the reader to truly 'feel' the poems.

What remains constant is her emotional stance, each poem emerging from a place of strength even when tinged with rage or regret.  Whether admonishing a former lover, riffing on faith or reflecting on the state of our world, her words ring with passion and fortitude.

In "Reproach" she deftly conjures the agony of being more used than loved: "Who offered you my temple / to harness at your whim, / to perform your drunken ritual / and embalm me from within?"

And in "Come Healing II" she harmoniously extends Cohen's prayer through one of her own: "Oh undivided Love, / undivided Faith / come healing of the spirit / in every blessed way. / Come healing of the spirit / that bids each nation rise, / come healing of the sorrow / dripping from each love-torn eye."

Hoofprints On The Moon is poetry to be read, re-read, savoured and shared.

*~ Ian French (IF the Poet), Canadian Individual Slam Poetry Champion 2014 - www.ifthepoet.com*

**Previous Poetry Collections by Ronda Wicks Eller**

Creative Misinterpretations (Collaborative Poems with Daniel Kolos and Filomena Pisano), 2017, HMS Press, London, Ontario, Canada ISBN: 978-1-55253-087-0

The Lion and the Golden Calf, 2008, SkyWing Press, Clinton, Ontario, Canada ISBN-13: 987-0-9809335-0-5

Songs in the Aurora Borealis, 2005, HMS Press, London, Ontario, Canada ISBN: 1-55253-060-4

My Harmonic Perfection, 1995, HMS Press, London, Ontario, Canada ISBN: 1-895700-022-1

Ronda's website:
https://rwicksellercwg.wixsite.com/home

"Dance of One" was published in 'My Harmonic Perfection'.

No other poems in this collection have been previously published.

www.ingramcontent.com/pod-product-compliance
Lightning Source LLC
Chambersburg PA
CBHW022029090426
42739CB00006BA/342